The Name of the Lord is...

Volume One: Pretty Awesome, Great, Glorious and Like Totally Excellent!

By: Stephen Olar

Print ISBN: 978-1-926461-03-8

Electronic ISBN: 978-1-926461-04-5

Dedication

I dedicate *The Name of the Lord is... Volume 1 – Pretty Awesome, Great, Glorious and Like Totally Excellent* to Gary Hawes, In recognition of 45 years of faithful service as the Director of Michigan Christian Campus Ministries (wwwhhcf.org). His faith, vision, love and example touched, influenced and blessed the lives of thousands of students – myself included. Relationships do indeed begin with a name. Congratulations on this milestone, Gary. God bless you in your future endeavors.

Picture from www.hhcf.org.

Contents

The Name of the Lord is...

ALL RIGHT I ADMIT IT

Occasionally I watch that TV show about hoarders. I shake my head in disbelief at the scenes of ruined houses, packed full of what has become useless junk and garbage and I realize that I am just as bad.

Now when you come to my house, you will not see piles of stuff all over the place that has been there for ages. There is no rotting food in the cupboard (although I won't vouch for the fridge). I don't frequent yard sales looking for some trinkets or prized treasure nor do I obsess over collecting things which aren't all that rare and valuable.

I am a hoarder of information. There, I've said it. I store away facts, snippets of information and peruse used bookstores for out of print copies by my favorite authors. I've got more training than I know what to do with and am constantly on the prowl to learn new things. People stopped playing Trivial Pursuit with me because I am a walking encyclopedia of trivial stuff.

My lovely wife glares at me every time I bring another book home. I tell her I always have space for books. Of course having a library card helps, because I can borrow and enjoy them for a while without having to squeeze them into my already over stuffed milk crates.. er... shelves... yeah... shelves.

The computer made life easier. I got rid of a lot of files, documents and other stuff that had been living in filing cabinets for decades; stuff like my school notes from college – all of them – early writing attempts and boxes of magazines. I even had special small filing cabinets full of material from Radio Bible Class, which sends you all of this free stuff!

Then I obtained a tablet. I was never a big fan of them until I learned something important about them. They can contain hundreds if not thousands of books. Then I discovered another wonderful thing; F-R-E-E electronic books. Isn't that wonderful!

I have a recipe box full of cards with information on them. I have been working on this project for about 10 years now. As I read through the Bible and came across a name or title for God, I would jot it down with a few other notes and then file it away thinking that someday I would like to write a book about the Names of God.

The Name of the Lord is...

Well, that someday has arrived, but it is going to take more than one book to talk about all the names and titles of God, not to mention this one, which is made up of phrases that start with "The name of the Lord is... "

So in a flash of inspiration, the name of the book and the others in the series is based upon that phrase.

In our western culture, the significance and meaning of a person's name is rarely as important as they were in biblical times. Names meant something. They could be in reference to a historical event, relate to a prophecy, honoring a character or aspect of God or based upon a physical attribute.

More importantly, I have been reminded about the importance of knowing someone's name.

Gary Hawes was the Director of Michigan Christian Campus Ministries and when I attended Lake Superior State University, well, College when I was there... It kind of grew up. Gary also served as our Campus Minister. He would make the 5 hour drive from his home near Lansing, Michigan to Sault Ste. Marie every week.

Gary would start off his talk almost the same way every week. He would ask two questions. The first one he would ask us was to introduce our selves and then ask another question like "What is the name of your favorite take out place?"

There were usually 60 or 70 people who attended the weekly meetings. The regulars knew the real point Gary was about to make. We would introduce ourselves and then answer the question of the evening. As people around the room answered the questions some of us were hard at work remembering the names of all those people.

After the last person had introduced him or herself, Gary would sit back in his chair and ask for a volunteer to name off everyone in the room. The person would then go around and attempt to name everyone. It was surprising how high the success rate and we would often applaud and congratulate the person.

When he or she had named the last person, Gary would say something like, "We retain and remember a lot of information, but think about this: A relationship begins with a name."

Isn't that so very true? When we want to get to know a person better, especially if we want to date them, the first thing we attempt to find out about them is their name. It would be rather awkward if we called someone "Hey, you!" and then ask them on a date. We want to build a relationship with them and we start with "Hi! My name is... What's your name?"

Knowing God is really no different.. He wants us to know Him, so He gave us His names to consider. He knows our names, shouldn't we know His? His names and titles are a reflection of who God is: His attributes, character and reminders of what He has done and continues to do for us.

For those who have participated in my other studies will notice the format is a little different for the first volume. I usually design studies in such a way that will teach you, the participant, Bible study methods and techniques.

Now don't get too excited or disappointed as the case may be. In future volumes you will see my familiar type of Bible study style again. This first volume represents a departure from my usual style of Bible studies. While you will see the studies where you have to work to find the answers, most of these chapters/lessons are more devotional than diggable in nature. So instead of pulling out the big treasure hunting tools, like your concordance or atlas, you get to use your small tools, like looking up verses and comparing them to others.

As you work your way through this study you will notice you are already familiar with many of the terms we will be exploring. We sing them in our worship services on a regular basis.

So before we actually dig into what God's names are and what they mean, let's get our feet wet by looking at what the writers of the Bible had to say about His name.

One final note, a little like a PPS on a letter. When I refer you to do a word study I will reference the Strong's Concordance numbering. So if the word is an Old Testament word, I will be reference as "H." A New Testament word will be prefaced with a "G."

I Lied... I could have just rewritten this but it looks more dramatic this way... Um.. yeah.

The Name of the Lord is...

He has sent redemption to His people;
He has commanded His covenant forever:
Holy and awesome *is* His name.
Psalm 111:9

Lesson One

Our God is an Awesome God! (And so is His Name)

Yes, He certainly is!

The late Rich Mullins signature song has become an anthem of worship for millions of Christians since its release in 1988. What is interesting, however, is most people sing the chorus and tend not to sing the verses, which describe how awesome He really is.

When we are singing about God being awe-inspiring, and declaring our respect and reverence for His name we don't think about the other side of the coin of *awesome*. The original meaning of the word which comes from Old Norse to the English language meant *to fear*.

Before we even start our study, and without consulting a dictionary, what is your definition of the word awesome.

Now look up the definition in a dictionary and record it here.

Complete the *Word Summary* for Awesome. H3372

To see how the word is used in various versions, fill out the *Comparison Chart*. The versions you will be looking at are: King James (KJV) New King James (NKJV), New International Version (NIV), The Message and one other version of your choice. And no, you cannot repeat a version. So you don't have to stand in the bookstore and open a bunch of Bibles or go to the library, you can access multiple versions at biblegateway.com or biblestudytools.com. I have completed a line as an example.

You will notice there are five extra spaces on the chart. This word is used over 300 times. It is up to you to look up five of them and add them to the chart.

What did you discover about this word that you may not have been aware of before?

Look over your investigations and create a definition of awesome which takes all the different meanings into consideration..

What can you take away from this lesson on the word awesome?

Complete the following statement. Now I will use my teacher voice here: you have to create a complete thought. No one word answers please. Feel free to add a couple of sentences.

The name of my God is awesome because...

Word Summary Date of Study:

Word:	Verse:_____
Strong's Number:	

Definition:

Times Used: ___ Translated as:

Other Sources	Definition(s)

Other Bible References	How Used

Putting it in My Own Words

Takeaway

Compare the Words

Verse	KJV	NKJV	NIV	The Message	
Psalm 111:9	Reverend	Awesome	Awesome	Worthy of our respect	Terrifying (NOG)
Psalm 99:3					
Daniel 9:4					
Malachi 1:14					
Deuteronomy 28:58					
Exodus 15:11					

Additional Notes:

O LORD, our Lord,
How excellent *is* Your name in all the earth!
Psalm 8:9

Lesson Two

His Name is Excellent

As I studied out this lesson I was reminded of several cooking shows where celebrity chefs judging the dishes of contestants remark on identifying the layers of taste which were teasing their taste buds. There may be a sweet component, a sour one, a crunchy one and the list goes on.

The same can be said when you are studying the concepts words bring to mind. Some are a single note; only one meaning, while others have multiple meanings and nuances applicable to the framework of the context in which they are being used.

This is one of those words which seem layered with multiple meanings based upon context. It is such a versatile word there are two Hebrew words which are translated excellent.

Sometimes when I am studying such a word I will often create my own paraphrase or expanded version using the different meanings. A lot of time I will get an entirely different picture of this word.

Before we even get into the meaning of these words write down your definition of excellent. Preferably you will not be using the dictionary to do this. Write out what your own meaning.

Let's take a look at the first word. Complete the *Word Summary* for H117.

What did you discover about this word?

The Name of the Lord is...

List the verses with the ways this word is used.

Considering the conclusion you may have reached concerning this word. What would be your definition of this word? Provide some examples of how your definition/s would work in a sentence.

Ok, let's take a look at the other word. H7682. You know the drill.

What did you discover about this word?

What are the ways it is used?

What is your definition of this word when you consider all of its meanings?

Pretty Awesome, Great, Glorious and Like Totally Excellent!

Complete the *Comparison Chart* for these two words.

What are the similarities?

What are the differences?

Take a look at Psalm 8:1. In light of what you have learned about the word H117 write the verse with each of the meanings. When you do this, what does it add to your understanding of excellent?

Now do the same with Psalm 148:13 (H7682). How does this change your understanding of the word excellent?

Why is the name of the Lord Excellent?

Complete the following sentence.

I declare the name of the Lord to be excellent because...

Word Summary Date of Study:

Word:	Verse:_____
Strong's Number:	

Definition:

Times Used: ___ Translated as:

Other Sources	Definition(s)

Other Bible References	How Used

Putting it in My Own Words

Takeaway

Word Summary Date of Study:

Word:	Verse:_____
Strong's Number:	

Definition:

Times Used: ___ Translated as:

Other Sources	Definition(s)

Other Bible References	How Used

Putting it in My Own Words

Takeaway

Comparison Summary

VS.

	Scripture	

Insight:

Takeway:

Pretty Awesome, Great, Glorious and Like Totally Excellent!

Additional Notes:

The Name of the Lord is...

And blessed *be* His glorious name forever!
And let the whole earth be filled *with* His glory.
Amen and Amen. Psalm 72:19

Lesson Three

Glorious is His Name

Like many of the words we are exploring in this study, there are multiple meanings which can be applied. Once again we have two words to look at. There are some differences to them which add layers of understanding and will give us a deeper appreciation when we sing this word in our worship services.

It is sometimes funny how the same word can mean different things. One of the words we will be looking at has a range of meanings from honor to fat or heavy. So as we think about this... why would a word that is used to talk about glory also have the connotation of heaviness or honor?

This word is H3513. Complete the *Word Summary* for this word.
What are the primary and secondary definitions of this word?

What are the ways this word is translated? Include the references in your answer and remember the list may vary depending on the version you are using.

Take a look at Deuteronomy 28:58. Complete the *Event Summary* for this verse. Remember to take into consideration the context of the passage.
Why does Moses encourage the people to observe and obey the Law?

What was a surprise to me is this word also has a negative connotation to it. Look up Exodus 8:15 and 1 Samuel 6:6.

What is the negative connotation of this particular word?

What do we call it today? (Hint Proverbs 18:12)

Let's leave that word for a moment and examine our other word. Complete the *Word Summary* for H3519

What does this word mean?

Complete the *Comparison Chart* for these two words.
What are the notable differences?

Read Psalm 66:1-7 and complete the *Poetry Worksheet*. For those of you who are not familiar with studying poetry I have included a bonus chapter from **The Bible School Dropout's Guide to More Bible Study** courtesy of the author. No, wait... that's me. My bad. There goes that gratuitous self-promotion thing again. Darn. Did you hear the riddle about how many writers does it take to change a light bulb? Think about it and I may tell you the answer near the end of this lesson or in another one to encourage you to keep on reading...

What did you notice about our word in this passage?

Although we have been focusing on making his name glorious, what does thinking about how we are to "Sing out the honor of His name" imply? What are the subtle differences between honor and glory in our society today?

What did you learn from your time in Psalm 66:1-7?

Pretty Awesome, Great, Glorious and Like Totally Excellent!

In looking at both words, create an expanded definition of the word glorious?

Treasure Hunt!

Pull out your concordances and let's explore the Bible. The two words are used over 315 times. Look up 10 of those times...er... verses which talk about other ways we are to glorify God. List them here and please include the references, the what or the why. I may want to stop by for tea and see what you've written. Or better yet, go to my website (bibleschooldropout.com) and share them with others.

1.
2.
3.
4.
5.
6.
7.
8.
9.
10.

Complete the following statement:
The name of the Lord is glorious because...

Bonus: How many writers does it take to change a light bulb?
Forget about the light bulb! Let me tell you about my book!

Word Summary Date of Study:

Word:	Verse:_____
Strong's Number:	

Definition:

Times Used: ___ Translated as:

Other Sources	Definition(s)

Other Bible References	How Used

Putting it in My Own Words

Takeaway

Event Summary

Date of Study:

Passage:	Title:	
Time:	Location:	**Support**
Details		
Details from Other Passages		
Details from Other Sources		
Spiritual or Practical Principles		
Take away		

Word Summary   Date of Study:

Word:	Verse:_____
Strong's Number:	

Definition:

Times Used: ___ Translated as:

Other Sources	Definition(s)

Other Bible References	How Used

Putting it in My Own Words

Takeaway

Poetry Summary   Date of Study:

Passage	Title:	
Historical Context:		

Verse:	Images:	Support

Insight from the Context:	

Insight from Other Scripture or Sources	Source

Takeaway:

Comparison Summary

VS.

	Scripture	

Insight:

Takeaway:

Additional Notes:

The Name of the Lord is...

Let them praise Your great and awesome name—
He *is* holy.
Psalm 99:3

Lesson Four

Meditate on the Significance of His Name

Great is an adjective which modifies a noun with a particular quality. When we use it to describe God's name we are indicating there is something significant or important about it. Well of course there is something significant and important about God's name. Not to mention noble, proud and mighty as well.

Complete the Complete the Word Summary for H1419.

What is the base definition of the word translated Great?

Complete the Poetry Summary for Psalm 99.
According to this Psalm why is the name of the Lord great? Give specific examples from the passage.

Now complete the Poetry Summary for Psalm 76.
According to this Psalm why is the name of the Lord great? Give specific examples from the passage.

The Name of the Lord is...

Now we are going to go on a treasure hunt. Record ten more verses which talk about how great God is. Record the reference and what it says.

1.

2.

3.

4.

5.

6.

7.

8.

9.

10.

What have you learned about the word great which you may have not been aware of before?

Complete the following phrase.
The name of the Lord is great because...

Word Summary Date of Study:

Word:	Verse:_____
Strong's Number:	

Definition:

Times Used: ___ **Translated as:**

Other Sources	Definition(s)

Other Bible References	How Used

Putting it in My Own Words

Takeaway

Poetry Summary

Date of Study:

Passage	Title:

Historical Context:

Verse:	Images:	Support

Insight from the Context:

Insight from Other Scripture or Sources	Source

Takeaway:

Poetry Summary   Date of Study:

Passage	Title:

Historical Context:

Verse:	Images:	Support

Insight from the Context:

Insight from Other Scripture or Sources	Source

Takeaway:

Additional Notes:

Glory in His holy name;
Let the hearts of those rejoice who seek the LORD!
Psalm 105:3

Lesson Five

Bless His Holy Name

Here is one of those words which we have a vague churchy concept of and sing of on a regular basis but many of us do not have a solid grasp on what it really means to worship a holy God. This word is actually used a lot in the Bible. It not only refers to God, but to us as His children and what is expected of us; but that is a whole different study.

The concept of holy is not a concrete one. There are many layers of meanings which are applied not only to God but to things, such as the tabernacle and temple to people. It can only deepen our worship experience when we understand why His name is holy.

Without pulling out or up a dictionary write down what you think the word holy means.

Complete the Word Summary for holy H6944
What is the basic meaning of the word holy?

Since the basic meaning of the word holy is to set apart what does it mean when we set apart the name of the Lord?

What are some of the other uses of this word? Don't forget to include the references.

The Name of the Lord is...

Complete the Poetry Summary for Psalm 105:1-6
According to this passage what are some of the reasons we should recognized the holiness of God's name?

What did you learn about this word that you may have not known?

Is your definition of the word holy different than it was at the beginning of this lesson?

Write out your new definition of the word holy.

Complete the following phrase.

I declare God's name to be holy because...

Word Summary Date of Study:

Word: Strong's Number:	Verse:_____
Definition:	
Times Used: ___ Translated as:	

Other Sources	Definition(s)

Other Bible References	How Used

Putting it in My Own Words

Takeaway

Poetry Summary

Date of Study:

Passage	Title:

Historical Context:

Verse:	Images:	Support

Insight from the Context:

Insight from Other Scripture or Sources	Source

Takeaway:

Additional Notes:

The Name of the Lord is...

I will praise You forever,
Because You have done *it;*
And in the presence of Your saints
I will wait on Your name, for *it is* good.
Psalm 52:9

Lesson Six

It is Good to Give Thanks

It seems we have been spending a lot of time examining the Psalms. This lesson is not going to change that. We have another wonderful word to look at and explore. The word *good* can mean a range of ideas from morally excellent, to righteous to quality.

So let's dig a little bit deeper and attempt to determine its meaning and ideas are. Of course this does mean you will have to do more word studies (and Poetry Summaries). Just think about it though: How much fun is to discover the various levels of meaning of this word and how it will enhance your understanding of God?

I knew you would see it my way...

Let's take a closer look at the word translated *good*. Complete the *Word Summary* for H2896.

How many times is this word used in the Old Testament?

How many times is it translated *good*?

I'm not going to make you look up every single reference, but I would like you to look up 10 references and explain how this word is used in each reference. That should give us a general idea of meaning.
1.

2.

3.

4.

5.

6.

7.

8.

9.

10.

Complete the *Poetry Summary* for Psalm 52.
What does this verse have to say about the goodness of God's name?

Read Through Psalm 92.
Make a list of why it is good to give thanks to the Lord and praise His name.

Now that we have had a chance to examine this word, what is your upgraded definition? And no, you cannot write out your original definition.

Pretty Awesome, Great, Glorious and Like Totally Excellent!

What did you learn about this word that you may have not known before?

Complete the following statement.
The name of the Lord is good because...

Word Summary   Date of Study:

Word:	Verse:_____
Strong's Number:	

Definition:

Times Used: ___ Translated as:

Other Sources	Definition(s)

Other Bible References	How Used

Putting it in My Own Words

Takeaway

Poetry Summary

Date of Study:

Passage	Title:

Historical Context:

Verse:	Images:	Support

Insight from the Context:

Insight from Other Scripture or Sources	Source

Takeaway:

Additional Notes:

His name shall endure forever;
His name shall continue as long as the sun.
And *men* shall be blessed in Him;
All nations shall call Him blessed.
Psalm 72:17

Lesson Seven

As Long as the Sun Shines

Sometimes a manufacturer will offer a lifetime guarantee on a product they are selling. It seems like a good deal, but then when you read the fine print, there are conditions which must be meant in order to make a claim that they will offer.

Yaweh made a similar guarantee based on the power of His name alone. The difference of His guarantee is the time: His warranty is valid forever.

There are two words we are going to start our study with today.

Complete *Word Summaries* for the following words.
H5769
H1961

What did you discover about the word forever?

What insights did you gain from your study of the word endure?

The Name of the Lord is...

You have already visited our next stop on our journey in the last chapter. Take a look at your notes from your time in Exodus 3. Notice the same verse where you found the word memorial, you should also notice the declaration that Name is forever.

What was God Planning to do?

Why would God declare His name is forever in this passage?

Read Psalm 72 and complete the *Poetry Summary*.
What did you discover about why David declared The Lord's name is forever?

Complete the *Poetry Summary* for Psalm 135 and record what you discovered about why the writer declared the Name of the Lord is forever.

Why do you think the word endures was added to forever?

Why is it significant that the name declared to be forever is Yaweh (LORD) in these passages?

Complete the following phrase.
I declare the name of the Lord will endure forever because...

Word Summary Date of Study:

Word:	Verse:_____
Strong's Number:	

Definition:

Times Used: ___ Translated as:

Other Sources	Definition(s)

Other Bible References	How Used

Putting it in My Own Words

Takeaway

Word Summary   Date of Study:

Word:	Verse:_____
Strong's Number:	

Definition:

Times Used: ___ Translated as:

Other Sources	Definition(s)

Other Bible References	How Used

Putting it in My Own Words

Takeaway

Poetry Summary   Date of Study:

Passage	Title:	
Historical Context:		

Verse:	Images:	Support

Insight from the Context:

Insight from Other Scripture or Sources	**Source**

Takeaway:

Poetry Summary   Date of Study:

Passage	Title:	
Historical Context:		
Verse:	**Images:**	**Support**
Insight from the Context:		
Insight from Other Scripture or Sources		**Source**
Takeaway:		

Pretty Awesome, Great, Glorious and Like Totally Excellent!

Additional Notes:

The Name of the Lord is…

This *is* My name forever, and this *is* My memorial to all generations.'
Exodus 3:15 b

Lesson Eight

Standing on Holy Ground

Do you remember your first encounter with God?

Some people testify it was quite dramatic, like Moses' experience. Sometimes experience was quiet and subdued. But one thing is sure; I doubt we will ever forget that encounter. For many of us it was a life changing experience.

Let's begin our examination of this topic by defining our word. Please fill out the *Word Summary* of H2143.

What did you discover about this word and how it is used?

How is it used in relation to other aspects of God?

Read Exodus 3:1-15 and complete the *Narrative* and *Event* Summaries.
What is happening?

What is the issue Moses is having with this conversation with God?

What does God offer to resolve Moses' concerns?

The Name of the Lord is...

Why do you think God has declared His name to be a memorial?

What is the name God uses in this passage to identify himself?

Read Hosea 12:2-6. Complete the *Narrative Summary*.
What event is the prophet referencing?

Describe the encounter Jacob had with God as retold in this passage.

What is the name Hosea declares is memorable?

What point does Hosea want us to know about remembering the name of the Lord?

Read Psalm 135 and complete the *Poetry Summary*. Please note the word we are studying appears in verse 13, but it may not be translated as memorable.
What information does this Psalm provide as to why we consider the Lord's name as a memorial?

What is the specific name used in this Psalm?

In the three passages we have examined the writers referred specifically to the designation we call Jehovah or Yaweh. In considering the events described in the passages why do you think this name is the one that is declared at least once by God to be memorable?

At the beginning of this lesson I asked if you remembered you first encounter with God. After working your way through this study, write at least one paragraph about that experience. Use the *Additional Notes* page for your answer.

Pretty Awesome, Great, Glorious and Like Totally Excellent!

What makes God's name memorable?

What works has God done in your life to make His name memorable?

Complete the Following phrase.
The Lord's name is a memorial in my life because...

Word Summary Date of Study:

Word:	Verse:_____
Strong's Number:	

Definition:

Times Used: ___ Translated as:

Other Sources	Definition(s)

Other Bible References	How Used

Putting it in My Own Words

Takeaway

Event Summary

Date of Study:

Passage:	Title:	
Time:	Location:	Support
Details		
Details from Other Passages		
Details from Other Sources		
Spiritual or Practical Principles		
Take away		

Narrative Summary

Date of Study:

Passage:	Title:	
Type of narration: Story, Account, Chronology, Information, Backfill		
Characters:	Theme:	

Details:	Support

Principles:	Illustrates:

Summary:

Takeaway:

Narrative Summary

Date of Study:

Passage:	Title:

Type of narration: Story, Account, Chronology, Information, Backfill

Characters:	Theme:

Details:	Support

Principles:	Illustrates:

Summary:

Takeaway:

Poetry Summary   Date of Study:

Passage	Title:	
Historical Context:		
Verse:	**Images:**	**Support**
Insight from the Context:		
Insight from Other Scripture or Sources		**Source**
Takeaway:		

Additional Notes:

The Name of the Lord is...

Praise the LORD, for the LORD *is* good;
Sing praises to His name, for *it is* pleasant.
Psalm 135:3

Lesson Nine

How Delightful and Lovely is His Name

This is another one of those adjectives which describe a particular quality to something, in this case the name of the Lord. Well come to think of it, most of our study is about these adjectives.

I came across this little gem on my way to investigating some other aspect of God's name and quickly made note of it. The downside of this is the only reference which declares the name of God is pleasant. Depending on the version you are using, this will be translated, lovely, sweet, gracious, pleasing, beautiful delightful and the list keeps growing.

One of the sources I used in preparing this study indicated it is used of people who are a joy to be around. Hmm… It also carries the idea of something that is sweet sounding, like some good ol' Southern Gospel (Capitalized to emphasize its importance) (Baker).

I'm going to have to stop there, because if I continued, this would turn into a sermon and that would defeat the purpose of studying it out and discovering some treasure for your own.

The word we are exploring will be H5273. Please complete the *Word Summary*.
What have you discovered about this word?

Now please complete the *Poetry Summary* for Psalm 135.
List the reasons why this Psalm declares the Lord's name is pleasant, or whatever translation you are using.

Since this word is only used 13 times in the Old Testament (You should know that as you have studied it) look up the other references (yup... should have done that too) and record how it is being used in each passage.

1.

2.

3.

4.

5.

6.

7.

8.

9.

10.

11.

12.

What have you discovered about this word that you may not have been aware of before?

Complete the following phrase.
The Name of the Lord is pleasant because...

Word Summary Date of Study:

Word:	Verse:_____
Strong's Number:	

Definition:

Times Used: ___ Translated as:

Other Sources	Definition(s)

Other Bible References	How Used

Putting it in My Own Words

Takeaway

Poetry Summary   Date of Study:

Passage	Title:	
Historical Context:		
Verse:	**Images:**	**Support**
Insight from the Context:		
Insight from Other Scripture or Sources		**Source**
Takeaway:		

Additional Notes:

The Name of the Lord is...

Oh, magnify the Lord with me,
And let us exalt His name together.
Psalm 34:3

Lesson Ten

Exalt His Name!

Here is another of those words we use on a regular basis in our worship services. But do we really understand what it means to exalt someone?

Other than the songwriter, the average churchgoer sings the words, usually standing and sometimes hands upraised without knowing what it means. It's just one of those words which sounds worshipful and belongs in a song directed towards God. We sing it out as part of our worship experience.

I am not saying this because I want to sound superior or some sort of religious know-it-all. I count myself as one of those people who also sing the words without thinking about what they really mean. I had a good idea of what exalt means, but this study helped to clarify the wonderful nuances of its definition.

 Let's start with the first word. Complete the *Word Summary* for H7311
What are the different ways this word is translated?

Complete the *Verse Summary* for Psalm 34:3
Here is a list of the Strong numbers:
Magnify H1431
The LORD H3068
Exalt H7311
Name H8034
Together H3162

When you have completed the Verse Summary, write out your own amplified version of this verse.

What did you learn about this word?

Now let's take a look at the next word. Complete the *Word Summary* for H7682.

Complete the *Comparison Chart* for these two words.

In what ways are they the same?

How does this word differ from the first word?

Complete the *Verse Summary* for Psalm 148:13
The Strong's word numbers are:
H1984
H8034
H3068
H3588
H905
H7682
H1935
H5921
H776
H8064

Paraphrase this verse using the definitions you have discovered.

Pretty Awesome, Great, Glorious and Like Totally Excellent!

What does it mean to exalt someone or something? Include primary and secondary meanings and don't forget to give examples.

What is something you learned about this word that you may have not known before you started this study?

Complete the following statement:
I exalt the name of God because...

Word Summary   Date of Study:

Word:	Verse:_____
Strong's Number:	

Definition:

Times Used: ___ Translated as:	

Other Sources	Definition(s)

Other Bible References	How Used

Putting it in My Own Words

Takeaway

Verse Summary

Date of Study:

Title:	
Verse:	
Strong's Number and Definition(s)	**Used Elsewhere**
Quotation? Yes No	**Summary of Original Passage**

Summary of Verse in Context

Putting it in My Own Words

Takeaway

Word Summary Date of Study:

Word:	Verse:_____
Strong's Number:	
Definition:	
Times Used: ___ Translated as:	

Other Sources	Definition(s)

Other Bible References	How Used

Putting it in My Own Words

Takeaway

Comparison Summary

VS.

	Scripture	
Insight:		
Takeaway:		

Verse Summary

Date of Study:

Title:	
Verse:	
Strong's Number and Definition(s)	**Used Elsewhere**
Quotation? Yes No	**Summary of Original Passage**

Summary of Verse in Context

Putting it in My Own Words

Takeaway

Additional Notes:

The Name of the Lord is...

The name of the LORD *is* a strong tower;
The righteous run to it and are safe.
Proverbs 18:10

Lesson Eleven

A Place of Refuge

I knew it was time to write another Bible study because of a certain song that kept rolling around in my mind. I would find myself mentally singing the words, humming the words, tapping my fingers in beat to the music only I could hear. I am unable to quote the song here unless I pay a licensing fee, but the song is based on Proverbs 18:10.

I am *glad* I have memorized this verse a long time ago. It is my go to verse when the storms of life are crashing and booming all around me. It brings me a sense of calm to know the center of my life is not only a rock but a place of refuge and comfort.

Complete the *Verse Summary* of Proverbs 18:10.
How is the name of the Lord described here?

What is the name of the Lord contrasted to in verse 11?

Read Luke 12:13-21.
Generally what do wealthy people tend to put their faith in?

Why do you think this?
How does Proverbs 18:12 fit into this picture?

What is the definition of Strong from verse 10?

What are some other ways this word has been translated?

What can we learn from the following verses? Don't forget to take in the context of the passage.
Psalm 61:3

Psalm 71:7

Psalm 78:26

Isaiah 49:5

Now it's time to dust off your concordance. Look up five more reference referring to God's strength. Record them here as well as what the verse states about God's strength.

What image(s) does the word *tower* bring to your mind?

From your *Verse Summary*, what is the definition of *tower*?

Share some examples from the Bible which illustrate was a tower is and does.

What is the definition of the word safe from your Verse Summary?

Comment on the following verses on how they expand upon your definition of safe.

Psalm 59:1

Psalm 69:29

Psalm 91:14

Isaiah 33:4-5

Using the information you have discovered, write out an expanded paraphrase of Proverbs 18:10.

Complete the following statement.

For me the name of the Lord is a strong tower because…

Verse Summary

Date of Study:

Title:	
Verse:	
Strong's Number and Definition(s)	**Used Elsewhere**
Quotation? Yes No	**Summary of Original Passage**

Summary of Verse in Context

Putting it in My Own Words

Takeaway

Additional Notes:

The Name of the Lord is...

And He shall stand and feed *His flock*
In the strength of the LORD,
In the majesty of the name of the LORD His God;
And they shall abide,
For now He shall be great
To the ends of the earth;
Micah 5:4

Lesson Twelve

Consider the Majesty of His Name

The line of the song goes "Worship His Majesty (Hayford)." Here again we have one of those churchy words we sing about all the time, but we really don't know what the word means when we acknowledge the majesty of the Lord.

When you sing that song are you referring to getting your pride on? How about declaring the excellency of the Lord (and his Name)? Maybe it's about the pomp or display of his power? Perhaps you are indicating He is somewhat arrogant? Well perhaps not arrogant in a negative sense...

So let's begin by recording what you think the idea(s) the word majesty convey. Remember: No turning to Webster for an answer.

Complete the *Word Summary* for the word translated majesty. H1347

What are the positive meanings for this word?

What are the negative meanings of the word?

The Name of the Lord is...

How would you tell the difference when you read them in verses? (Hint: it begins with a "con" and ends with a "text.")

When we study Micah 5:4 in context, what type of literature is the passage a part of?

Complete the *Observation Summary* and *Prophecy Summary* for the passage Micah 5:1-15.

What are the details of the prophecy?

Who was it originally directed at?

What verse in this passage is quoted in the New Testament?

What is the verse referring to?

Pull out or concordance and do a search for the word majesty. How is this word used to describe God?

What have you discovered about this word you may not have been aware of before?

Complete the following sentence.
I declare the majesty of God's name because...

Word Summary   Date of Study:

Word:	Verse:_____
Strong's Number:	

Definition:

Times Used: ___ Translated as:

Other Sources	Definition(s)

Other Bible References	How Used

Putting it in My Own Words

Takeaway

ument flow:

Observations

Date of Study:

Passage:	Focus:

Asking: Who ☐ What ☐ When ☐ Where ☐ Why ☐ How ☐

Reference:	Statement:

Insight:

Observations

Date of Study:

Passage:	Focus:

Asking: Who ☐ What ☐ When ☐ Where ☐ Why ☐ How ☐

Reference:	Statement:

Insight:

Prophecy

Date of Study:

Passage:	Title:
Speaker:	Audience
Fulfilled? ☐ yes ☐ no when Fulfilled:	Thesis:

Symbols	Represents	Support

Figures:	Represents	Support

Passage in Context:
Purpose(s) of the Prophecy:
Takeaway:

Additional Notes:

The Name of the Lord is...

For our heart shall rejoice in Him,
Because we have trusted in His holy name
Psalm 33:21

Lesson Thirteen

A Name to be Trusted

This is an interesting word. Well… they all are. Like so many words we use on a daily basis, we don't give much thought to what the meaning of the word is.

What do we mean when we say we trust someone? Is it an endorsement of confidence in that person? Is it a declaration of hope and reliance? Are we declaring a level of security and expectations in the person we trust?

That is something you should have an answer for by the end of this lesson. Come on now… Did you really think I would make it that easy for you?

Without resorting to a dictionary write out what you think the meaning of trust is.

Complete the Word Summary for Trust. H982
What kind of a word is this? Ei. Is it a noun, or a verb?

How is this word used in Scripture? Record your findings with the references.

What is an in depth definition of the word trust?

The Name of the Lord is…

Complete the Poetry Summary for Psalm 33:16-22

What are some things we learn about the Lord and why we can place our trust in Him?

Let's go on a treasure hunt! Complete the Treasure Hunt chart. There are ten verses listed. Record the reasons we have to trust God. There are also ten blank spaces for you to add ten of your own verses.

What are some of the reasons we have to put our trust in God's name?

Has your definition of the word trust changed? Explain why you have reached this conclusion.

Complete the following statement:
I trust the name of the Lord because…

Word Summary Date of Study:

Word:	Verse:_____
Strong's Number:	
Definition:	
Times Used: ___ Translated as:	

Other Sources	Definition(s)

Other Bible References	How Used

Putting it in My Own Words	

Takeaway	

Poetry Summary

Date of Study:

Passage	Title:

Historical Context:

Verse:	Images:	Support

Insight from the Context:

Insight from Other Scripture or Sources	Source

Takeaway:

Additional Notes:

The Name of the Lord is…

Pretty Awesome, Great, Glorious and Like Totally Excellent!

But let all those rejoice who put their trust in You;
Let them ever shout for joy, because You defend them;
Let those also who love Your name
Be joyful in You.

Psalm 5:11

Lesson Fourteen

Love is a Verb...

It kind of surprised me to discover the first thing about this word is the fact it is a verb and not a noun. A verb is action oriented. It means we are doing something. But what?

I realize that in English the word can be a noun or a verb depending on the context of how it is used. But there is no mistaking the difference in Hebrew. There is one verb and three noun forms.

When you consider the verse at the beginning of this lesson, what definition comes to mind?

Complete the *Word Summary* for H157
What did you discover about the word love as an action word?

Read Isaiah 56:1-8 and complete the *Prophecy Summary*.

This is what we would classify as a dual fulfilment prophecy.

The Name of the Lord is...

Who is Isaiah referring to in the short term?

What evidence do you have to support those who are in view in the short term?

Who is Isaiah referring to in the long term?

What evidence do you have to support the ones who are in view in the long term?

What actions to the outsiders do to demonstrate their love and devotion to God?

What are God's promises to those people?

What references can you find in the New Testament which contained similar promises?

Complete the *Poetry Summary* for Psalm 5.

What is the attitude of a person who loves the name of the Lord?

According to this Psalm why do we love the name of the Lord?

Pretty Awesome, Great, Glorious and Like Totally Excellent!

What is the promise to those who love his name in Psalm 69: 36?

What have you discovered about the word love?

What did you learn about loving the name of the Lord?

Complete the following phrase.
I demonstrate love for the name of the Lord by...

Word Summary Date of Study:

Word:	Verse:_____
Strong's Number:	

Definition:

Times Used: ___ Translated as:

Other Sources	Definition(s)

Other Bible References	How Used

Putting it in My Own Words

Takeaway

Prophecy

Date of Study:

Passage:	Title:
Speaker:	Audience
Fulfilled? ☐ yes ☐ no when Fulfilled:	Thesis:

Symbols	Represents	Support

Figures:	Represents	Support

Passage in Context:

Purpose(s) of the Prophecy:

Takeaway:

Poetry Summary   Date of Study:

Passage	Title:	
Historical Context:		

Verse:	Images:	Support

Insight from the Context:

Insight from Other Scripture or Sources	**Source**

Takeaway:

Additional Notes:

The Name of the Lord is…

Praise the Lord!
Praise the name of the Lord;
Praise *Him,* O you servants of the Lord!
Psalm 135:1

Lesson Fifteen

Let's have a Celebration!

This is something we all like to do! I don't know about you, but I never get tired of praising the Lord. I can sing anywhere and anytime of Jesus. Sometimes I even sing out loud... when I'm alone or in a group where no one can really hear me.

When I think about how some Christians worship, it is not quite a celebration... it's more like a funeral. When they (not including myself in this one...) pull out their dusty old hymn books to sing songs written 200 years ago (Well that's a tad stretching it.. but I'm attempting to make a point.) and then sing those songs looking like they've been sucking on dill pickles, there's something wrong.

There is nothing wrong with the songs, mind you. I enjoy singing the classic hymns. There is something wrong with the attitude.

'Nuff said... if I keep on talking...er... writing you won't have anything to discover for yourself. So let's explore the reason we praise the name of the Lord.

Of course we are starting at the place we almost always do... with the word.
What is your definition of the word praise? And this is YOUR definition, not copied from dictionary.com.

The Name of the Lord is...

Ok let's take a look at the word translated as praise. Please complete the *Word Summary* for H1984.

What are the ways this word is used? Supply the reference with your answers.

What English word to we have which came from this word?

Complete the *Poetry Summary* for Psalm 113.

What are the reasons given for which we should be praising the Lord?

When we consider this word in our praise of God, what is the attitude we should be displaying?

There is a second word which is also translated praise. Please complete the *Word Summary* for H3043.

Depending on the version or translation you are using, how many times is this word used?

How many times does it refer to praise?

How many times does it refer to thanks?

Read through Isaiah 25. List the reasons why we praise the Lord.

Pretty Awesome, Great, Glorious and Like Totally Excellent!

Guess what? That's right we have a third word which is translated praise. Complete the *Word Summary* for H2167.

How does this word enhance our understanding of praise?

Write out a new definition of the word praise base on the three words you have just examined.

Create your own psalm of praise and recorded on the *Additional Notes* page.

What did you learn about praise that you may not have known about before this study?

Complete the following statement.
I will praise the name of the Lord because...

Word Summary   Date of Study:

Word:	Verse:_____
Strong's Number:	

Definition:

Times Used: ___ Translated as:

Other Sources	Definition(s)

Other Bible References	How Used

Putting it in My Own Words

Takeaway

Word Summary Date of Study:

Word:	Verse:_____
Strong's Number:	
Definition:	
Times Used: ___ Translated as:	

Other Sources	Definition(s)

Other Bible References	How Used

Putting it in My Own Words

Takeaway

Word Summary   Date of Study:

Word:	Verse:_____
Strong's Number:	

Definition:

Times Used: ___ Translated as:

Other Sources	Definition(s)

Other Bible References	How Used

Putting it in My Own Words

Takeaway

Poetry Summary

Date of Study:

Passage	Title:	
Historical Context:		

Verse:	Images:	Support

Insight from the Context:

Insight from Other Scripture or Sources	**Source**

Takeaway:

Additional Notes:

Give to the LORD the glory *due* His name;
Bring an offering, and come into His courts
Psalm 96:8

Lesson Sixteen

Consider the Value of His Name

This word is actually related to one we studied earlier; glorious. One is a verb and the other a noun. You will have to do some work to find out which is which. Actually there are a couple of words we have looked which can be translated glory. One is usually translated praise.

Write out what you think the word glory means.

Complete the *Word Summary* for this word translated Glory. H3519

What is the main idea behind this word?

When we consider the basic meaning of this particular word is value, wealth or riches. How does this change our concept of giving God glory?

How is this different from say H1984 – (check out the lesson on praising the Lord's name) where we are instructed to brag about the Lord?

Complete the *Poetry Summary* for Psalm 66:1-7

What insight did examining this passage provide regarding providing honor to His name?

The Name of the Lord is...

Complete the *Poetry Summary* for Psalm 96.

Does this passage enhance what you discovered from Psalm 66?

What did this passage add to your understanding of the word glory?

According to Malachi 2:2 what is the warning to the priests if they do not bring glory to the Lord's name?

Why do you think this warning directed towards the priests and not to everybody?

So dust off your Bibles and Concordances...we are going on a treasure hunt! Look up ten verses which use this word and record what they have to say about the reason to value the name of the Lord specifically and bringing value and honor to the Lord generally.
1.

2.

3.

4.

5.

6.

8.

9.

10.

Now that you have had the opportunity to explore this word, what is the definition based upon your learning experience?

Complete the following phrase.

I give value to the name of the Lord because...

Word Summary   Date of Study:

Word:	Verse:_____
Strong's Number:	
Definition:	
Times Used: ___ Translated as:	

Other Sources	Definition(s)

Other Bible References	How Used

Putting it in My Own Words

Takeaway

Poetry Summary

Date of Study:

Passage	Title:	
Historical Context:		

Verse:	Images:	Support

Insight from the Context:

Insight from Other Scripture or Sources	Source

Takeaway:

Poetry Summary   Date of Study:

Passage	Title:	
Historical Context:		
Verse:	**Images:**	**Support**
Insight from the Context:		
Insight from Other Scripture or Sources		**Source**
Takeaway:		

Additional Notes:

The Name of the Lord is...

Now the LORD descended in the cloud and stood with him there, and proclaimed the name of the LORD.
Exodus 34:5

Lesson Seventeen

Shout it from the Mountain Top!

Even when we get older and face the risk of setting off the smoke alarm, we load our birthday cakes with candles and make a wish before blowing them out in one huge breath.

I had to put a stop from putting candles on my cake; I was afraid I would pass out before I could blow them all out.

Moses had a wish. His wish was something many of us have wanted as well. He wanted to see God. God had spoken to him from a burning bush, within a cloud, or just seemed to have conversations with Him. But Moses longed to see the God who had called him to be the leader of His people.

God answered Moses' wish in a matter of fashion. But what was interesting about the encounter was not the fact it was Moses proclaiming the name of the Lord it was God proclaiming His own name.

Complete the *Word Summary* for proclaim. H7121

What did you discover about the word proclaim?

Read Exodus 33:12- 23 and complete the *Narrative Summary*.
What is happening in this chapter?

What does God promise Moses?

The Name of the Lord is...

What is Moses' request?

What was God's response?

Now look at Exodus 34: 1-8 and complete the *Narrative Summary* for this passage
What is the event surrounding this action?

What additional information do we learn about God in this passage?

What proclamation does God make about His name?

What is Moses' response after hearing the Lord proclaim His name and His works?

Complete the *Proclamation Worksheet* for this lesson. For each declaration God made about his Character find a supporting reference in Scripture.
Now that you have completed the chart, what have you learned about God and His Character?

Complete the following phrase.
I Proclaim the name of the Lord because...

Word Summary Date of Study:

Word:	Verse:_____
Strong's Number:	
Definition:	

Times Used: ___ Translated as:	

Other Sources	Definition(s)

Other Bible References	How Used

Putting it in My Own Words

Takeaway

Narrative Summary   Date of Study:

Passage:	Title:	
Type of narration: Story, Account, Chronology, Information, Backfill		
Characters:	Theme:	

Details:	Support

Principles:	Illustrates:

Summary:

Takeaway:

Narrative Summary

Date of Study:

Passage:	Title:

Type of narration: Story, Account, Chronology, Information, Backfill

Characters:	Theme:

Details:	Support

Principles:	Illustrates:

Summary:

Takeaway:

God's Proclamations

Reference	Proclamation	Which Means	Supporting Scripture

Additional Notes:

The Name of the Lord is...

Yes, in the way of Your judgments,
O LORD, we have waited for You;
The desire of *our* soul *is* for Your name
And for the remembrance of You.
Isaiah 26:8

Lesson Eighteen

Our Desire

I had three chapters left on my working outline when I came across this little jewel. I could have chosen to not include it; there were other references in context with this study which I chose not to use as they will be covered in subsequent studies. However this particular aspect had not been planned into another study yet and so it is now a part of this study.

I was reminded of a story my mother told me. When I was a young child – probably about two or three years old, she had taken me to church. The Eucharist was underway when I spotted a picture of Jesus on the wall. Apparently I yelled out "My Jesus!" much to my mother's embarrassment.

I was too young to remember this incident and my mother stopped going to church for a while. My memories of going to church start at about nine and it wasn't in the same one where I made my "declaration of faith" at ten years old.

Let's start our treasure hunt by writing down your definition of desire.

Now complete the *Word Summary* of H8378.

What did you discover about what this word means and how it is used?

Read Isaiah 26:1-9. Complete the *Prophecy* and the *Didactical* summaries for this passage.

The Name of the Lord is…

What is the main idea of this passage?

Why is this passage a prophecy?

Has it been fulfilled in our present frame of reference?

When do you think this prophecy will be fulfilled?

Where do you think this prophecy will be fulfilled?

What are the longings of Isaiah's soul as a result of this prophecy?

What is/are the focus/es of this prophecy?

When does the prophet seek God?

Using the Additional Notes to record your findings look for ten verses which show our desire or craving for God.

Pretty Awesome, Great, Glorious and Like Totally Excellent!

What did you learn from the verses you have explored?

What will the people learn?

How will the people learn of God's righteousness?

If you were to read the next section of Isaiah 26, what would you learn about the wicked?

How many chances does He give them to accept Him?

What can we learn about God from this passage?

Complete the *Verse Summary* for Isaiah 26:8.

What did you discover from your examination of this verse?

Write out an amplified version of this verse. And no, you cannot copy out the verse from The Amplified Bible.

The Name of the Lord is...

What have you learned about seeking God as a result of this study?

Complete the following phrase.

My soul craves Your name, O Lord because...

Word Summary   Date of Study:

Word:	**Verse:**_____
Strong's Number:	

Definition:

Times Used: ___ **Translated as:**

Other Sources	**Definition(s)**

Other Bible References	**How Used**

Putting it in My Own Words

Takeaway

Prophecy

Date of Study:

Passage:		Title:
Speaker:		Audience
Fulfilled? ☐ yes ☐ no when Fulfilled:		Thesis:

Symbols	Represents	Support

Figures:	Represents	Support

Passage in Context:

Purpose(s) of the Prophecy:

Takeaway:

Didactical Summary   Date of Study:

Passage:		Title		
Author:		Thesis:		
Audience:				
Verse	Argument	Statement		Support
Insight				
Takeaway				

Verse Summary

Date of Study:

Title:	
Verse:	
Strong's Number and Definition(s)	**Used Elsewhere**
Quotation? Yes No	**Summary of Original Passage**

Summary of Verse in Context

Putting it in My Own Words

Takeaway

Additional Notes:

The Name of the Lord is...

Sing to the LORD, bless His name;
Proclaim the good news of His salvation from day to day.
Psalm 96:2

Lesson Nineteen

Bowing the Knee to His Name

It never ceases to amaze me when I look at a verse differently than I have done before and discover something totally new. When I explored the idea of blessing the Lord I thought it was something to do with praise (which it does), feeling thankful, (which it also does) and speaking highly of the object or person we are blessing (which it does as well).

We also have the concept that blessing someone or something is saying a benediction loaded with words of goodwill. Maybe our concept of blessing is this, but the Bible appears to support a slightly different concept. I could go on but then... spoilers... you know.

Without resorting to a dictionary, what is your definition of the word *bless*?

Complete the *Word Summary* for the word *bless*. H1288
What did you learn about this word?

Complete the *Poetry Summary* for Psalm 100.

What are the reasons it gives to bless the name of the Lord?

The Name of the Lord is...

Instead of doing a Poetry Summary on six or seven Psalms, which I know you really, really want to do; take out your Bible (make sure you dust it off) and look for ten verses. You can look for more if you want. You are looking for reasons to bless the Lord. Use the *Additional Notes* page to record your findings.

What you learned about blessing the name of the Lord?

What did you learn about the word bless which you may have not known before?

Complete the following phrase: I bless the name of the Lord because...

Word Summary   Date of Study:

Word:	Verse:_____
Strong's Number:	

Definition:

Times Used: ___ Translated as:

Other Sources	Definition(s)

Other Bible References	How Used

Putting it in My Own Words

Takeaway

Poetry Summary   Date of Study:

Passage	Title:
Historical Context:	

Verse:	Images:	Support

Insight from the Context:

Insight from Other Scripture or Sources	Source

Takeaway:

Additional Notes:

The Name of the Lord is…

Pretty Awesome, Great, Glorious and Like Totally Excellent!

Doubtless You *are* our Father,
Though Abraham was ignorant of us,
And Israel does not acknowledge us.
You, O Lord, *are* our Father;
Our Redeemer from Everlasting *is* Your name.

Isaiah 63:16

Lesson Twenty

Our Redeemer from Everlasting

OMG!

No, really... OMG!

Most, if not all of us who are familiar with the cyber world have seen this exclamation when chatting or texting to people. It has been around a lot longer than that. But it is not actually associated with an exclamation of praise to God but rather an expression of surprise or disbelief.

Well, if you are not saying OMG! In praise and worship by the end of this lesson, then you need to go back to lesson one and review everything you have studied to this point.

Most Christians today have a vague to void concept of who a kinsmen-redeemer (KR) was and the duties they were obligated to perform if they accepted the role. The most we get from the KR is the story of Ruth and how Jesus redeemed us like Boaz did for Ruth.

Well... there is much more to the story, or to mix our metaphors a bit... Ruth is only the tip of the iceberg.

Complete the *Word Summary* for redeemer. H1350

What are some of the different ways this word is used? Please write down the references.

What is the definition of redeemer?

Complete the *Topical Summary* for KR.

What is a KR?

What are the qualifications of a KR?

Read through Ruth 3:1-4:12. Record the steps from Ruth's request to Boaz's solution to the situation.

Look up the following references which demonstrate the various duties a KR may be called upon to do. Record your findings.

Leviticus 25:25-28; Jeremiah 32:6-9

Leviticus 25:47-55

Genesis 38:8-10; Deuteronomy 25:5-10

Pretty Awesome, Great, Glorious and Like Totally Excellent!

Numbers 35:16-21

What do the following verses have to say about God as our redeemer?

Exodus 6:6-7

2 Samuel 7:22-24

Job 19:25

Job 19:25

Isaiah 43:1-7

Isaiah 54:5-8

Jeremiah 50:33-34

Scripture declares God as our redeemer, but according to Levitical Law, was that the most important qualification for someone to be a **kinsman** redeemer? (there is a hint hidden in this question...wink, wink)

According to Galatians 3:13-14 and 4:4-7 how did God resolve this requirement?

The Name of the Lord is...

How does Jesus qualify to be our redeemer?

Read Hebrews 2:5-18. What does this passage indicate how Jesus became qualified to become our Kinsman Redeemer?

According to Isaiah 63:16 how long has God name been Redeemer?

Complete the following statement.

I declare the name of God as Redeemer because...

Word Summary   Date of Study:

Word:	Verse:_____
Strong's Number:	

Definition:

Times Used: ___ Translated as:

Other Sources	Definition(s)

Other Bible References	How Used

Putting it in My Own Words

Takeaway

Topical Summary   Date of Study:

Title:	Topic:
Scripture:	Theme:

Key words/phrases:

Verses	Points	Support

Takeaway

Additional Notes:

The Name of the Lord is...

...whoever calls on the name of the Lord
shall be saved...
Joel 2:32b

Lesson Twenty-one

There is only one name

This is what it is all about.

During the course of this study we have explored the reasons we should praise the name of the Lord. You may have noticed we have been primarily exploring the Old Testament at this point. The reason for this is the beginning of a series which will be exploring the Old Testament names of God.

However, many of you have already reached the conclusion we can also apply what we are studying to Jesus Christ, and you would be right.
What is significant about the passages we are going to be studying in this lesson is Paul quotes this verse in Romans 10:13; in effect saying that the name of Jesus Christ is whom we call upon for salvation.

This is not the first time an apostle made such a claim. Peter said in Acts 4:12, "Nor is there salvation in any other, for there is no other name under heaven given among men by which we must be saved."

It is clear from the Scriptural record Peter, Paul and the other apostles acknowledge that Jesus Christ was the Messiah and it was only on the power of His name salvation is granted to those seeking Him.

Oops... spoilers.

As you know with me it's all about the words and this one is no different. Now depending on your translation the word we are exploring may be saved or delivered or even escape. So let's take a look at H4422. Don't forget to complete the Word *Summary*... bet you thought I forgot about that little detail, didn't you?

What did you learn about this word?

What are the other words that are translated for this word?

Write out Joel 2:32 in an amplified or expanded style.... And no you are not allowed to copy down the verse from the Amplified Bible. You may have to complete the Verse Summary in order to do that.

What did writing an expanded version of this verse change when from its normal length and words?

Take a look at the following verses and write down the common thought in them.

Isaiah 43:11

Isaiah 45:21

Hosea 13:4

What is the common thought of these three verses?

What does the word savior mean? H3467

Why is that significant when you think about what Joel said and Paul quoted?

What is the meaning of Jesus name?

What is the Hebrew equivalent?

Pretty Awesome, Great, Glorious and Like Totally Excellent!

How does that connect to Peter's declaration in Acts 4?

Record at least one thing you did not know about our topic today.

Complete the following phrase.
The name of the Lord has the power to save because...

Word Summary Date of Study:

Word:	Verse:_____
Strong's Number:	

Definition:

Times Used: ___ Translated as:

Other Sources	Definition(s)

Other Bible References	How Used

Putting it in My Own Words

Takeaway

Verse Summary

Date of Study:

Title:	
Verse:	
Strong's Number and Definition(s)	**Used Elsewhere**
Quotation? Yes No	**Summary of Original Passage**
Summary of Verse in Context	
Putting it in My Own Words	
Takeaway	

Additional Notes:

Appendices

The following chapters on poetry and prophecy are from The Bible School Dropout's Guide to More Bible Study - First Edition © 2010 by Stephen Olar. ISBN 1451539916/EAN-13 9781451539912

Works Cited

The Name of the Lord is...

A Poem by any Other Name

It is often said that art is in the eye of the beholder. I've seen some art that wouldn't behold in my eyes as art and yet they are considered masterpieces.

One example in Canada which raised eyebrows, was a painting purchased by the National Art Gallery of Canada. This "work of art" was nothing more than a blue canvas with a red stripe painted down the middle. The name of the painting; "*Voice of Fire*." It created a firestorm all right. The purchase cost several million taxpayer dollars. There was much criticism about the waste of taxpayers' money when anybody with a paint brush and two cans of latex paint could have done the same thing for under a couple of hundred bucks. The curators of the art museum vigorously defended their choice and the furor eventually died down.

The moral of the story is this: Don't buy with other people's money what you wouldn't buy for yourself! And of course P.T. Barnum's famous comment, "There's a sucker born every minute," fits the bill, too!

Poetry is to the literary world what art is to the visual world. It expresses the highest thoughts and deepest emotions of humans. As a result, the author often uses highly imaginative or figurative language to convey those thoughts.

When we think of poetry, the first thing that comes to mind is it rhymes and follows a rhythmic pattern of speech.

Roses are red

Violets are Blue

Sugar is sweet,

But not as sweet as you.

Hebrew authors did not use this style of writing in their poetry. As common to many eastern cultures, the poetry was written more to provoke the human intellect and make the audience consider the words of the writer.

The Name of the Lord is…

Instead of a rhythmic pattern, most Hebrew poetry was written in a parallel or symmetrical pattern. The author states a though in the first line and then restates it in the second line.

Each line is called a stitch or a colon. The couplet formed is called a distitch.

Proverbs 1:20

"Wisdom calls aloud outside;

She raises her voice in the open square"

If the author carried his though over into a third line, then the form is called a tristitch.

Psalm 1:1

"Blessed is the man

Who walks not in the counsel of the ungodly

Nor stands in the path of sinners,

Nor sits in the seat of the scornful;"

Hebrew poetry rarely added a fourth line. Perhaps the author said all he had to say in 3 lines and wasn't interested in creating a quad-stitch; or maybe a cross-stitch.

When you read Job, Psalms, Proverbs, Song of Solomon, Ecclesiastes, and Lamentations, you will notice this pattern. It doesn't mean the author was drinking and forgot what he had just written, but that was the form in which they expressed their thoughts.

You may be surprised to know that this form wasn't only limited to poetry and songs. About half of the Hebrew Old Testament is written in a similar manner (Poetry, 1979).

Take a look at Genesis 1:1-2 where you can see a parallel idea presented.

"In the beginning God created the heavens and the earth.

The earth was without form, and void; and darkness was on the face of the deep. And the Spirit of God was hovering over the face of the waters."

Even when you compare Genesis chapters one and two, you see the author repeats some of the details of the first chapter and goes into greater detail of what happened on the sixth day.

You can classify parallelisms several ways. The first is the author is basically restating the first though in the second line. This is called *synonymous parallelism.*

Psalm 2:4

"He who sits in the heavens shall laugh;

The Lord shall hold them in derision."

The author may also emphasize his point by stating the opposite in the second line from what he stated in the first in an *antithetic parallelism.* You can usually identify this structure because the second line begins with the words "but" or "nor."

Proverbs 15:1

"A soft answer turns away wrath

But a harsh word stirs up anger."

The author may use a second or third stitch in the restatement in order to clarify or complete the thought he wrote in the first line. This is *synthetic parallelism.*

Psalm 49:16-17

"Do not be afraid when one become rich,

When the glory of his house is increased

Fore when he dies he shall carry nothing away;

His glory shall not descend after him."

Climatic parallelism is when the author expresses the end result in the second line from his actions which he stated in the first.

Psalm 32:5b

"I said, "I will confess my transgression to the LORD,"

And You forgave the iniquity of my sin."

Finally, *emblematic parallelism* is built upon a figure of speech. Generally one line is figurative, the other literal. This form is also usually synonymous since the second line describes the same thing as the first (Sterrett, 1974).

Psalm 42:5

"As the deer pants for the water brooks,

So pants my soul for You, O God."

When Poetry is not really Poetry, but it's still called Poetry

Huh??

When you study this particular type of literature, it is important to keep in mind that not all Hebrew Poetry is recorded in Psalms, nor could it be classed a strictly poetry. Nor is it restricted to only what we classify as wisdom literature, which includes Job, Proverbs, Ecclesiastes, Song of Solomon and Lamentations.

Let's take a look at a few examples, and hopefully clear things up.

Judges 14:14

And he said unto them,

Out of the eater came forth meat,

And out of the strong came forth sweetness.

And they could not in three days expound the riddle.

The riddles we pose in our cultural generally do not follow a pattern. For example: What is a hamburger's favorite bed? Answer: A bed of lettuce!

Ezekiel 19:1-3 shows the prophet used this style in recording an allegory.

Moreover take thou up a lamentation for the princes of Israel,

And say, "What is thy mother?"

A lioness: she lay down among lions,

she nourished her whelps among young lions.

And she brought up one of her whelps:

it became a young lion,

and it learned to catch the prey; it devoured men."

The Name of the Lord is...

Even God has been known to throw out a stitch or two. Take note of His proclamation in Genesis 25:23:

"And the Lord said to her:

'Two nations are in your womb,

Two peoples shall be separated from your body;

One people shall be stronger than the other,

And the older shall serve the younger.'"

Songs were also written in this style. Take a look at a part of the Song of Moses in Exodus 15:1b-2.

"I will sing to the LORD, For He has triumphed gloriously!

The horse and its rider He has thrown into the sea!

The LORD is my strength and song,

And He has become my salvation;

He is my God, and I will praise Him;

My Father's God, and I will exalt Him."

The song of Deborah in Judges 5:2-3 (Notice how she made use of the apostrophe...)

"When the leaders lead in Israel,

When the people willingly offer themselves

Bless the Lord!

Hear, O kings!

Give ear, O princes

I, even I, will sing to the LORD;

I will sing praise to the LORD God of Israel."

This style of writing was very popular with the writers of the Old Testament, so expect to see it often as you journey through its pages.

Guidelines for Interpreting Poetry

So now that you know absolutely way more about Hebrew poetry that you ever wanted to, the question is what to do with it once you've decided to study it. Here are several guidelines to help.

1.   Remember that most poetry is highly figurative. That doesn't mean we throw out our rules regarding literal interpretation. Since the language is figurative, you have to think about what the imagery suggests to arrive at a conclusion.

      Psalm 42:1

      "As the deer pants for the water brooks,

      So pants my soul for You,"

Give yourself a minute to consider the picture. You have a thirsty deer, perhaps being chased, perhaps during the dry season where water is scarce, looking for refreshment. The writer has set the scene of the longing he has to experience God, just like that thirsty deer is driven to seek water.

2.   Look for clues to help you understand what circumstances the poem may have been written or even give you an idea about when it was written.

Psalm 42:4

"For I used to go with the multitude;

I went with them to the house of God,

With the voice of joy and praise,

With a multitude that kept a pilgrim feast."

From this verse, we know the temple in Jerusalem was in existence and the author would often join the people coming to the city to celebrate one of the several yearly feasts in the Jewish calendar.

Psalm 42:6b

"...from the land of Jordan,

And from the heights of Hermon

From the Hill Mizar"

From this verse, the author tells us that he is currently living near Mount Hermon, the location of the head waters of the Jordon River.

Psalm 42:3

"While they continually say to me,

'Where is your God?'"

This verse indicates the author was facing ridicule or persecution for holding on to his beliefs.

These are all clues to help understand the motivation of the author as to why he was writing this particular Psalm.

3.   Don't be dogmatic. Rather than "lay down the law" poetry expresses the authors' feelings, and emotional state. He is not attempting to teach doctrine. Although you can use this literature to illustrate spiritual concepts, it should not be used to form the basis of doctrine.

4.   Poetry is design for meditation. That doesn't mean you sit in the lotus position chanting the passage over and over again. The idea of mediation is to think about it, study it, pray it, talk about it. Take a walk and think about the words and what the author is attempting to convey from his heart to the paper.

5.   Your conclusions should naturally flow from the context of the Psalm or the passage you are studying. You should be able to support your conclusions with other passages of Scripture. As you are studying this passage, can you think of other passages of Scripture which talk about the same concepts?

Putting the Plan into Action

The chart which goes with this lesson is designed to assist you by letting you focus on the things you need to help you in your study. You don't need to start at the top and work your way down.

The Name of the Lord is...

For instance, you probably won't have a title for your study until you are near the end of it. Depending on what you discover, you may go to the historical context by reading what was happening when the piece was written. You may discover additional insight from the cross references you also examine.

Use the chart to study Psalm 42. The passage section is for you to make your general observations. We work to answer the questions who, what, where when why and how.

I'm going to walk you through the process, but I want you to make your own notes as we work together to draw some conclusions about this passage.

First of all, does the Psalm make any mention of the person who wrote it? What is he saying about himself?

We learn the following information:

1. He describes himself as a son of Korah.
2. He reckons his longing for God as a search to quench his thirst. (vs. 1)
3. He desires to experience God and has been unable to do so.(2)
4. His separation from God is very bitter.(3)
5. He remembers the times when he participated in corporate worship of the feast pilgrims. (4)
6. He gives himself a prep talk to continue hoping in God and praising Him.(5)
7. He seems to be in a place of exile. (6)
8. He will remember God where he is now. (6)
9. He is being oppressed by his enemies. (9-10)

Ask these questions as you go over your notes:

1. What is his desire?

2. Why is he unable to seek God?

3. What are his circumstances?

4. How does he lift himself from his despair?

What does he say about other people?

God:

1. Is to be sought after. (1)
2. Is a living God. (2)
3. Is a help for the countenance. (5, 11)
4. May be pouring out judgment. (7)
5. He will command His loving kindness during the day. (8)
6. He gives a song in the night. (9)
7. He is a rock (9)

As you look at these observations, ask yourself the following questions:

1. What does "countenance" mean?

2. Why did the writer refer to God as the living God?

3. What are the promises the writer claims from God?

4. Why does the writer refer to God as his Rock?

His enemies:

1.   Continually say to him, "Where is your God?"
2.   The reproach or oppress him.

The multitudes:

1.   Went into the House of God with the voice of Joy and praise. (4)
2.   They were pilgrims to the city to observe the feast.

Can you determine what has happened or is happening in this passage?

1. The writer may be in some form of exile. (4, 6)
2. The writer may be experiencing some form of judgment.(7)

Other than this information, all we can determine is the writer is unable to go to Jerusalem. We don't know why this is. So it may not be helpful in studying this psalm.

We also have several locations mentioned in this Psalm.

1.   The house of God (4) – This is a reference to the temple, which was located in Jerusalem.
2.   The land of the Jordan
3.   Mount Hermon
4.   Hill Mazar.

These passages refer to real places. Where are they in relation to Jesrusalem? Can you answer the question if the author is actually where he says he is, or is he likening his spiritual "exile" like a physical one?

Does the passage give a reference to time?

1. When he remembers these things, he pours out his soul. (4)
2. Because the writer was at the temple, we know it was in existence during that period. (4)
3. He is oppressed all day long by his enemies. (10)

You should also be on the lookout for repeated words and phrases. For instance, Verses 5 and 11 are repeated. This tells us this Psalm has 2 verses. Are they talking about the same thing? Are they different and how are they Different?

Verses 1-5: Appear to be talking about the longing the writer has to experience the closeness of God. In his time of exile, he remembers being in God's presence in the temple.

Verses 6-11: The writer appears depressed, he remembers the goodness of God and the reason he has to hope in his Rock. As William MacDonald said in *The Believer's Bible Commentary*, "He may not be able to go to the house of God, but he can still remember the God of the house (MacDonald, 1989)!"

Now that you have made some observations from the context, can you find any cross references which talk about similar ideas?

For instance:

References about the soul thirsting for God:

"O God, You are my God;

Early will I seek You;

My soul thirsts for You;

My flesh longs for You

In a dry and thirsty land

Where there is no water"

Psalm 63:1

"My soul longs, yes even faints

For the courts of the LORD;

My heart and my flesh cry out for the living God."

Psalm 84:2

"I spread out my hands to You;

My soul longs for You like a thirsty land.

Selah."

Psalm 143:6

"Blessed are those who hunger

and thirst for righteousness,

For they shall be filled."

Matthew 5:6

Do these verses add any insight to what you are studying? Look at the promise Jesus made to those who hunger and thirst after righteousness. How does this compare with what the writer said in 42:7-8?

Take a look at Jeremiah's words in Lamentations 3:22-26.

"Through the LORD's mercies we are not consumed,

Because His compassions fail not.

They are new every morning:

Great is your faithfulness.

"The LORD is my portion," says my soul,

"Therefore I hope in Him!"

The LORD is good to those who wait for Him,

To the soul who seeks Him.

It is good that one should hope and wait quietly

For the salvation of the LORD."

Does this particular passage help to explain the reason why the writer of Psalm 42 chooses to hope in God and continues to praise Him in spite of the circumstances he finds himself in?

As you examine your cross references, they help you to gain greater understanding to the mind of this particular psalmist, his circumstances and his state of mind. Take note of your observations in the section "Answers from other passages."

What are some of the insights you have gained from your study. What is the psalmist attempting to convey in his words? What feelings is he expressing? What is his deepest longing? Record your insight on the chart under "My insight."

With any Bible study, the most important part is asking yourself the question, "What does it mean to me?" What are the principles God is working to reveal to your spirit and how do you respond to them?

Psalm 42 shows many things. It reveals the longing we have to experience God in a personal way. We want to talk with Him, even if it is to tell Him we don't feel Him.

The author tells us that our past experiences and knowledge of God can tide over the bad times. He also shows that in spite of the circumstances we find ourselves in, we can fully place our trust in God. He demonstrates His loving kindness towards us and gives a song to lighten our load in the darkest night

The psalmist reminds himself, and us that God is our Rock. That word for rock can mean a fortress or a stronghold. He is our place of refuge. This is a place of security, trust and hope.

What does this Psalm mean to you?

Wrapping it up!

Studying the poetry of the Bible can be an eye and spirit opening experience if we stopped to consider what the author was saying. In today's world, we are often in too much of a hurry to just sit and think about it or to take the time needed to spend in God's word. God commands us to meditate on his Word. Think about it. Roll it over in your mind. Ponder the significance of what is being said.

A lot of the psalms we know in bits and pieces, as modern songwriters use them as launching pads for the messages they want to convey. However God has His own message He wants to convey to us. In a world of instant messaging, e-mails and wireless communication, God is speaking His heart to us when he said, "Be still, and know that I am God."

Poetry Summary

Date of Study:

Passage	Title:

Historical Context:

Verse:	Images:	Support

Insight from the Context:

Insight from Other Scripture or Sources	Source

Takeaway:

The Name of the Lord is…

Prophecy - History Pre-written

Most of us today would like to know what the future holds. There is a booming business in astrology, tarot cards and other psychic attempts to discern future events. The Bible is one of the oldest prophetic records known. Many of its predictions cover thousands of years and many are still waiting to be fulfilled.

The study of prophecy, or eschatology (the "official" theological term), fascinates many. Often new believers want to deep dive into the book of Revelation even before they have had the opportunity to ground themselves in the basics of their new faith or learn sound bible study methods. As a result, they get bogged down in all of the symbolism they come across and either get discouraged or go off on all sorts of rabbit trails that have no support from the rest of Scripture.

A serious Bible student should not ignore importance of prophecy. When it was written over 25% of the Bible was prophetic in nature. Many people describe prophecy as history pre-written. As you study your Bible, you will see how many prophecies were fulfilled exactly as they were predicted. It is also important to understand the nature of prophecy, its purpose, its characteristics and apply a consistent method of study in order to come to conclusions that are in line with the rest of Scripture (remember the word "context").

Many doomsday cults that are in operation today are the result of misinterpretation, misunderstanding and misapplication of predictive Scripture. Even society in general has mistakenly termed end of the world as "Armageddon."

We often read of psychic predictions of disasters which came to pass, as predicted. There are many people who claim to prophesy in God's name, yet God condemns these forms of prophecy, calling them false prophets, and the work of demons and spirits. Take a look at the following verses:

"There shall not be found among you anyone who makes his son or his daughter pass through the fire, or one who practices witchcraft, or a soothsayer, or one who interprets omens, or a sorcerer, or one who conjures spells, or a medium, or a spiritist, or one who calls up the dead. For all who do these things are an abomination to the LORD, and because of these abominations the LORD your God drives them out from before you." Deuteronomy 18: 10-12

"And the L<small>ORD</small> said to me, "The prophets prophesy lies in My name. I have not sent them, commanded them, nor spoken to them; they prophesy to you a false vision, divination, a worthless thing, and the deceit of their heart.""

Jeremiah 14:14

"Beloved, do not believe every spirit, but test the spirits, whether they are of God; because many false prophets have gone out into the world." 1 John 4:1

The penalty for false prophecy was rather sever; you were stoned, and I don't mean with a joint! *"A man or a woman who is a medium, or who has familiar spirits, shall surely be put to death; they shall stone them with stones. Their blood shall be upon them."* Leviticus 20:27

Defining Prophecy

The *Encyclopedia of Biblical Prophecy* describes prediction or prophecy as "an announcement ... of the future...which is beyond the power of the human mind to discern or calculate (Payne, 1973)."

The Old Testament word for prophecy, *Nawbi,* simply means a spoken or written prediction. *Propheteia,* the New Testament equivalent, means basically the same thing. The people who uttered, wrote, or acted out these predictions, or prophecies were called prophets and seers. It was the job of these people to be the spokesperson for God. The word *prophe,* refers to a person who speaks on the behalf of another. In classic Greek culture, the prophet, seer, or oracle, was one who interpreted the will of some deity. The Oracle of Delphi, was a priestess who went into a trance proclaimed the will of Apollo, the Greek sun god.

In the Old Testament prophet was the person who was responsible for revealing God's will. His responsibilities also included reproving the people for their sins, counsel, guidance and encouraging people to repent and return to God.

The only true record of future events is contained within the pages of the Bible. That may read like a presumptuous statement (fancy word for arrogant, boastful, etc....), but it is based in biblical fact. God, because of who He is, is the only person who possesses knowledge of the future.

Behold, the former things have come to pass,

And new things I declare;

Before they spring forth I tell you of them.

Isa 42:9 MJKV

Thus says the LORD, the King of Israel,

And his Redeemer, the LORD of hosts:

I am the First and I am the Last;

Besides Me there is no God.

And who can proclaim as I do?

Then let him declare it and set it in order for Me,

Since I appointed the ancient people.

And the things that are coming and shall come,

Let them show these to them.

Do not fear, nor be afraid;

Have I not told you from that time, and declared it?

You are My witnesses.

Is there a God besides Me? Indeed there is no other Rock;

I know not one. Isaiah 44:6-8

The Purpose of Prophecy

To gain an understanding of predictive literature, we should take a look at it's purpose. There are several reasons God used predictions. When you are studying prophetic passages, it is important to keep these purposes in mind. It will help you to understand why the prediction was given and the circumstances in which it was given.

One of the main reasons God used predictions was as proof of who He was and who people were dealing with. In Isaiah 44:6-8 - God declared there were no other gods beside Him. Part of the proof of His existence, was His ability to proclaim things that shall come. Jesus said much the same thing when He spoke to His disciples the night before the crucifixion. *"Now I tell you before it comes, that when it does come to pass, you may believe that I am He."* John 13:19

God considers the ability to know the future a test for those who would claim godhood. A god or the representative of a god should have the foresight, and wisdom to demonstrate knowledge of the future.

Let them bring forth and show us what will happen;

Let them show the former things, what they were,

That we may consider them,

And know the latter end of them;

Or declare to us things to come.

Show the things that are to come hereafter,

That we may know that you are gods;

Yes, do good or do evil,

That we may be dismayed and see it together.

Indeed you are nothing,

And your work is nothing;

He who chooses you is an abomination.

Isa 41:22-24

Even from the beginning I have declared it to you;

Before it came to pass I proclaimed it to you,

Lest you should say, My idol has done them,

And my carved image and my molded image

Have commanded them.

Isa 48:5

A third aspect of the intent of prophecy was to indicate God's Will. In order prove to Saul that his kingship was from God, Samuel told him what would happen that day. David would know God's judgment for his sin of adultery and murder was going to be confirmed with the death of the child that had been the result of the tryst (1 Samuel 10:2-8, 2 Samuel 12:7-14).

For those who prophesied and their audience, prophecy was a test faith. Joseph was so sure God would deliver His people, he left instructions that his body was to be taken with them to the promised land (Genesis 50:24-25, Hebrews 11:22).

Prophecy was also an aid to faith. Jesus told His disciples, *"And now I have told you before it comes, that when it does come to pass, you may believe."* John14:29

Predictive literature provided assurance and comfort. Moses was presented with a sign that God would be with him on his mission to free the children of Israel. *"But Moses said to God, Who am I that I should go to Pharaoh, and that I should bring the children of Israel out of Egypt?*

So He said, "I will certainly be with you. And this shall be a sign to you that I have sent you: When you have brought the people out of Egypt, you shall serve God on this mountain."" Exodus 3:11-12.

To assure king Ahaz of the victory over Syria, this sign was given: *"So, the Lord Himself shall give you a sign. Behold, the virgin will conceive and shall bring forth a son, and they shall call His name Immanuel"* Isaiah 7:14

Prophecy was also used to motivate believers to live a life of holiness. *"We also have a more sure Word of prophecy, to which you do well to take heed, as to a light that shines in a dark place, until the day dawns and the Daystar arises in your hearts."*

2 Peter 1:19 MKJV

The main purpose of predictive literature was to point the way to the Messiah, Jesus Christ. There are over 100 prophetic passages in the Old Testament which specifically refer to the Messiah, His birth, work, death, resurrection, and reign.

"And He said to them, O fools and slow of heart to believe all things that the prophets spoke! Was it not necessary for the Christ to suffer these things and to enter into His glory? And beginning at Moses and all the Prophets, He expounded to them in all the Scriptures the things concerning Himself." Luke 24:25-27

"And He said to them, These are the words which I spoke to you while I was still with you, that all things must be fulfilled which were written in the Law of Moses and in the Prophets and in the Psalms about Me. And He opened their mind to understand the Scriptures" Luke 24:44-45

"You search the Scriptures, for in them you think you have eternal life. And they are the ones witnessing of Me." John 5:39

"Now to Him who is able to establish you according to my gospel, and the preaching of Jesus Christ according to the revelation of the mystery, having been unvoiced during eternal times; but now has been made plain, and by the prophetic Scriptures, according to the commandment of the everlasting God, made known to all nations for the obedience of faith;" Romans 16:25-26 MKJV

Characteristics of Prophecy

One of the first things about Bible prophecy is there is no set formula on how it was recorded, formatted, or specific pattern. It would have made things a lot easier when studying if all passages of prophecy started with "the following is a prediction." The closest we come is "Thus says the Lord…" Even then it is not always referring to a prediction!

Forms

Predictive literature comes in a variety of shapes and forms. Think of when we discussed different types of literature, like poetry, allegory, didactic (fancy for teaching), symbolism and more were all used. You will find prophetic passages take the form of spoken declarations, written records, dreams and visions. If that is not enough to keep you busy, some predictions were presented in the form of actions. Ezekiel and Hosea are examples of their actions rather than their words are the vehicle God chose to deliver His message. Let's take a look at some examples of predictive literature in the Bible.

Verbal declarations are the easiest to discover. The first was directly from God's mouth. *"And I will put enmity between you and the woman, and between your seed and her Seed; He shall bruise your head, And you shall bruise His heel."* Genesis 3:15

"So says Jehovah: For three transgressions of Damascus, yea for four, I will not turn away from it; because they have threshed Gilead with threshing instruments of iron." Amos 1:3.

It goes without saying the prophets kept written record of their predictions. Jeremiah had his prophecies burned by Jehoiakim (Jeremiah 36:32). Jeremiah turned around and wrote another book. Talk about dedication to his craft! *"So Jeremiah wrote in a book all the evil that would come upon Babylon, all these words that are written against Babylon."* Jeremiah 51:60.

Some prophecies were given in the form of actions, or object lessons. Ezekiel's declaration of the destruction of Jerusalem, how long the siege would last and the suffering of the people was acted out (Ezekiel 4-5).

Other prophecies took the form of dreams and visions. God warned Pharaoh in dream of the coming famine in Genesis 41 and Daniel records his vision of the future world empires in Daniel 8.

Time

When studying prophetic literature, you would think all of it would be in the future tense. After all, we are talking about events which had not occurred when they were predicted. Unfortunately that is not the case. Many prophets gave their messages as if they happening or had already occurred.

Studying Prophecy

The first thing we need to look for when we study prophecy is to be able to recognize it. It would be nice if every prophetic passage we look at started with a phrase like, "Prophetic Passage," or "Thus says the Lord about the future."

Take a look at the following passages. Can you tell which ones are considered prophetic? The answers will be supplied at the end of the lesson.

Genesis 50:25

Exodus :22-23

Daniel 1:18

Hosea 11:12

John 2:18-22

The biggest mistake people make when studying prophecy is to assume that since the passages are often figurative, they can change the way they interpret to a more subjective view, as figurative language is subjective by its very nature.

Nothing could be further from the truth. You will have less of a chance of making a mistake in your conclusion if you stick to the rules we have been using all along. Continue to use your normal method of interpretation and look for the plain sense of the passage. If it doesn't make sense normally, then move out and consider the literary device the author of the passage used. Many People automatically assume, for instance, that because Revelation is apocalyptic in nature, then normal or plain interpretation is no longer applicable and a more allegorical approach is justified.

Putting it into Practice

Let's take a look at a pretty familiar passage of Scripture. Daniel 2: 31-45.

Let's break it down

Verses 31-35:

"You looked, O king, and there before you stood a large statue--an enormous, dazzling statue, awesome in appearance.

The head of the statue was made of pure gold, its chest and arms of silver, its belly and thighs of bronze,

Its legs of iron, its feet partly of iron and partly of baked clay.

While you were watching, a rock was cut out, but not by human hands. It struck the statue on its feet of iron and clay and smashed them.

Then the iron, the clay, the bronze, the silver and the gold were broken to pieces at the same time and became like chaff on a threshing floor in the summer. The wind swept them away without leaving a trace. But the rock that struck the statue became a huge mountain and filled the whole earth. NIV

One of the things we need to look at this is the passage in its context. We learn the king was having a troubling dream, but was unable to remember it. So he calls for his advisors for assistance. They are unable to help them and in a fit of anger, the king threatens to kill them.

Daniel is able to intercede on behalf of the advisors and is able to interpret the dream for the king.

Because this is a dream, we can safely assume that the elements are figurative and symbolic. So now what we want to do is to identify what the symbols represent. So we are looking as a stature that starts with a head of Gold, and works its way to feet of clay and iron. Then a stone made without hands struck the feet of the statue, destroying it and filling the whole earth. What we want to know is what do all the separate elements means.

Lucky for us, Daniel explains all the details of the dream in verses 36-44!

Just to let you know, it won't always be that easy. Sometimes the prophecy is not totally clear on all the minute details. Take Revelation 11 for instance where we have John's vision of the two witnesses. The identity of the two witnesses is not made known. People have surmised they could be Enoch, Elijah, or Moses, but no one knows. Their identity is not important. But their message is.

Support or Cross references are your best friend when it comes to interpret a prophetic passage. We know Daniel's vision of the nations can be backed up by John in Revelation 17: 9-10, *"And here is the mind which has wisdom. The seven heads are seven mountains, on which the woman sits. And there are seven kings; five have fallen, and one is, and the other has not yet come. And when he comes, he must continue a short time."*

When we line this up with history, we understand that John is speaking of the world empires Egypt, Assyria, Babylonia, Media and Persian, and Greece. When John was speaking, the current empire was Rome. And there is one more world empire to come into existence. Daniel's vision starts with Babylon.

When we go back to the two witnesses in Revelation 11, we have a cross reference to Zechariah 4:2-14, these are the two that stand beside the Lord before the whole earth.

The context of the prophecy should also give you information on what the purpose of the prophecy was. In the Case of Daniel, God was informing Nebuchadnezzar, what His plans were concerning the kingdoms of the earth until He sets up His kingdom.

As always, the goal of your study is to determine what God wants us to know personally. What is the takeaway for you when you study this particular passage of Scripture?

Wrapping it Up

As we bring this lesson to a close, I cannot stress the importance of the need to stick to a consistent method of interpretation. Many assume that because of the highly symbolic and figurative nature of prophetic literature they can change their method of interpretation to a more subjective view.

By keeping to inductive Bible study methods, we can assure a more satisfactory conclusion to our study. We may interpret Scripture literally, but we also recognize symbolism and figures are used as a normal part of everyday language.

Understanding the role prophecy plays in the Bible, also gives us a solid framework as well. God had a specific reason for revealing the future to us, and that as nothing to do with people today who claim they can predict the future. Prophecy was given to us to show us who god is and what He is capable of doing. It also gives us a reason to have faith in Him and believe what He says.

Prophetic literature is without a doubt one of the more challenging portions of Scripture to study. However, don't let that stop you from discovering the jewels it contains.

Answers to which passages are prophetic

Genesis 50:25 - yes

Exodus :22-23 - yes

Daniel 1:18 – no

Hosea 11:12 - no

John 2:18-22 – yes

Prophecy

Date of Study:

Passage:	Title:
Speaker:	Audience
Fulfilled? ☐ yes ☐ no when Fulfilled:	Thesis:

Symbols	Represents	Support

Figures:	Represents	Support

Passage in Context:

Purpose(s) of the Prophecy:

Takeaway:

Works Cited

Baker, W. E. (2003). *The Complete Word Study Dictionary: Old Testament.* Chatanooga, TN: AMG Publisher.

Hayford, J. W. (n.d.). Majesty.

MacDonald, W. (1989). *The Believer's Bible Commentary elect. edition.* Nashville, TN: Thomas Nelson Publioshers.

(1979). Poetry. In *Encylcopedic Dictionar of Religion* (p. 2873). Washington, DC: Corpus Publications.

Sterrett. (1974). *How to Understand Your Bible.* Downer's Grove, Il: Intervarsity Press.

www.ingramcontent.com/pod-product-compliance
Lightning Source LLC
Chambersburg PA
CBHW081149090426
42736CB00017B/3237